# Many Plants, Many Places

by Cynthia Clampitt

PEARSON

Scott
Foresman

Editorial Offices: Glenview, Illinois • Parsippany, New Jersey • New York, New York
Sales Offices: Needham, Massachusetts • Duluth, Georgia • Glenview, Illinois
Coppell, Texas • Sacramento, California • Mesa, Arizona

ISBN: 0-328-13282-9

# CONTENTS

# Chapter 1: Plants for Each Place

Almost anywhere you go on Earth, you will see many kinds of plants. There are some places where the **climate** is so harsh that no plants grow there. You won't find plants living at the South Pole, for example, but most places support a variety of plant life.

Climate is one of the things that determine which plants grow in an area. Some places are warm all year, while some places have cold winters. **Annual** rainfall is another element of climate that affects plants.

Over thousands of years, plants slowly **adapted** to changing conditions. As wet places got drier or warm places got colder, small changes would help one plant survive, while another might not. In time, these small differences led to the growth of plants perfectly suited to very different climates.

Rain or snow, temperature, and the change of seasons help determine the types of plants that are successful in an area. Landforms and waterways also help determine which plants grow in an area. For example, mountains have very different plants than lakeshores.

In the United States, we have many different landforms and climate zones. The pictures below show the Northeast and the Southwest regions of the country.

**Northeast**

The Northeast has warm summers and cold winters. Plenty of rain falls there. Most of the Southwest has warm winters and hot summers, and little rain falls in much of this region.

Look at the two pictures. What differences do you notice? Where are plants greener? What clues show that there is less rain in the Southwest? Each place has plants that are perfect for its climate.

Southwest

### Ponds, Lakes, Rivers, and Oceans

Salt would kill most land plants, but plants in the ocean are suited to living in salt water.

Giant kelp, found in the cold waters of the North Atlantic Ocean, can grow as much as 14 inches per day. Giant kelp grows up to 100 feet long before it dies each winter.

Water lilies, shown below, live in fresh water, and are found in lakes, ponds, and rivers. Water lilies are suited to living in water. They have tough, waxy leaves that float and long stems that grow up from the soft mud below.

Because water lily leaves and flowers float, the stems do not have to hold them up. Instead, the stems are flexible, so they can move easily in water **currents.**

Reeds and rushes are water plants that grow near the water's edge. Only their roots and parts of their stems are under water.

Some water plants do not have roots at all. They get their **nutrients,** or food, directly from the water.

## Rain Forests

Some places have wet climates, with heavy rainfall. Forests that grow in these places are called rain forests. Washington's Olympic National Park rain forest often gets more than one hundred inches of rain in a year. The trees grow close together, so they grow tall to reach up to the sunlight.

Mosses and ferns are also suited to the rain forest. They are adapted for growing in the shade. Ferns and mosses grow beneath the trees—and even on the trees.

Red cedars and Douglas firs grow tall and close together in Olympic National Park rain forest.

## Deserts

Deserts are places that get less than ten inches of annual rainfall. Some deserts are cold, some are hot, but all are dry. Because rain is rare and often comes in short, heavy bursts, desert plants have to be able to either save water or grow quickly when water is available.

Some desert plants have spines, which are like thorns, instead of leaves. A cactus has its spines in star-like clusters. A spine has less surface area from which water can evaporate, or dry up. Desert plants also have **stomata,** or tiny openings on leaves or stems, that can close to keep water from evaporating.

The barrel cactus can expand to store water.

11

## Mountains

Mountains can be difficult places for plants to grow. High mountains can stop clouds, so all the rain falls on one side of the mountain. The other side may get very little rain, creating a dry climate. This effect is known as a rain shadow.

Strong winds may blow, which also dries a mountain's soil. The winds affect plants in other ways too. Many high mountains are cold as well as dry.

Of course, the higher up a mountain you go, the harsher the conditions. There are often great forests on the lower slopes of mountains, but the plants change as you climb.

Some mountain plants grow in clusters, that is, their stems grow close together. This traps heat and water. Often, plants grow close to the ground, which protects them from strong winds. Some plants, such as lichens, grow right on the rocks. Mountains in very hot regions may have many of the same plants you find in deserts.

▲ Lichens growing on rock

▼ Tree shaped by wind

## *Animals as Food*

Plants that live in places where the soil has few nutrients get what they need in other ways. Some of these plants actually eat insects and other small creatures!

The leaves of sundew plants have hairs that make a kind of glue. First, an insect gets stuck in the glue. Then, the leaf folds over the insect and traps it.

The pitcher plant has leaves that form tubes that are filled with liquid. The surface at the mouth of the tube is slippery. Insects slip and fall into the liquid and are digested by the plant.

Some consider the Venus's-flytrap to be the most interesting of the meat-eating plants. The Venus's-flytrap has leaves that are hinged in the middle. When an insect lands on one of the leaves, the leaf closes up, trapping the insect.

Pitcher plant

The Venus's-flytrap can trap and digest insects, such as this dragonfly, to get the nutrients it needs.

## Friends and Enemies

More common than plants eating animals is animals eating plants. For some plants, such as grass, the plant survives by growing back after the animal has moved on. However, many plants have thorns to protect them from animals. Others have leaves that taste bad or are poisonous.

Birds help spread seeds.

Plants and animals are not always enemies, however. Many plants need animals to help with their life cycles.

Juicy berries or other types of fruit attract bats, birds, monkeys, and other animals, which then spread the seeds far from the original plant. Beautiful flowers attract insects, which then spread pollen from one flower to another.

Just as different plants are specially suited to the climates in which they live, so too they are suited to the animals with which they live.

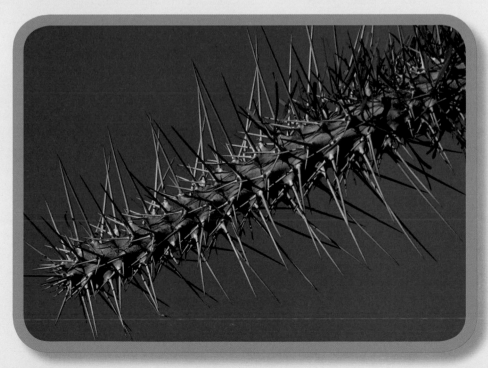

Thorns protect plants from animals.

# Now Try This

Plants need sunlight. Adaptations make it possible for plants to get the sunlight they need. This experiment will show you one of these adaptations.

**You'll need:**

- two small planting containers
- planting soil
- a shoebox
- two seeds (beans, corn, or other seeds)
- a small wedge or block

1. Put some soil in each container.

2. Plant a seed in each container.

3. Water both seeds a little.

4. Turn the shoebox on its side. Set the containers inside the shoebox.

5. Place the shoebox on a window sill, with the open side facing the window.

6. Put a block or a wedge under one of the containers. The container should be tilted away from the window.

7. Water the containers for a week or two.

8. Watch the seeds grow. Why do the stems grow differently? How does this help the plant get sunlight?

# Glossary

**adapted** *v.* to change to fit surroundings or conditions.

**annual** *adj.* in a year or for a year.

**climate** *n.* the kind of weather a place has year after year.

**currents** *n.* flow of water or air.

**nutrients** *n.* food needed by living things.

**stomata** *n.* small openings or pores in a plant or animal.